THIS WORKBOOK BELONGS TO:

the Biggest Alcoholic of the 21st Century

Copyright © 2018 Joanne Edmund

All rights reserved.

ISBN-10: 1719450358

Disclaimer

This book is not intended to be a substitute for medical advice or treatment. Any person with a condition requiring medical attention should consult a qualified medical practitioner or suitable therapist.

The information provided in this book is stated to be truthful and consistent, in that any liability, in terms of inattention or otherwise, by any usage or abuse of any policies, processes, or directions contained within is the solitary and utter responsibility of the recipient reader. Under no circumstances will any legal responsibility or blame be held against the publisher for any reparation, damages, or monetary loss due to the information herein, either directly or indirectly.

QUIT DRINKING

An Inspiring Recovery Workbook by a Former Alcoholic

Created by: Joanne Edmund

All rights reserved © 2018

Recovery doesn't happen in one day.
Or a few weeks.

It takes time.
But be aware, open your eyes, and it may start now.

Making small changes consistently
will always lead to bigger changes in life.

Dear Reader,

Thanks for purchasing my book.
I feel grateful to serve you with my carefully created workbook:
Quit Drinking

And I sincerely hope you enjoy, learn and find what you're looking for.

All the best,

Joanne Edmund

QUIT DRINKING

For my angels.

JOANNE EDMUND

A NOTE TO THE READER

I am not a doctor, not a therapist, not an AA counselor. I am a recovered alcoholic and I want to share the story of my recovery with you. To sincerely benefit all who commit to quit drinking. Since I was a young girl, I've wanted to be a writer. Fairy tales, in old books, seemed to tell of a world far away from my own.. A fine, fine world. Many years later, I am a grown-up woman and fairy tales still get me from time to time. Though the first book I'll publish is not one of kissing teenagers or magic elves, it's about the truth. About my addiction and what I did to overcome it. Now, under a pen name for substantial reasons, I am ready to make my dream come true. To become a writer. To tell you, the reader, that recovery, the fairy tale of every problem drinker, is not just a story. It is the one and final truth.

JOANNE EDMUND

CONTENTS

How To Use This Workbook	p. 17
Introduction	p. 19
My Background	p. 21
Chapter 1 - The First step	p. 29
Chapter 2 - Reconnect	p. 43
Chapter 3 - Meet Your Addiction, A Trusted Advisor	p. 51
Chapter 4 - A New Horizon	p. 59
Chapter 5 - A New Life	p. 65
Epilogue	p. 69
Book Recommendations	p. 73
Video Recommendations	p. 74
Quotes	p. 77
Affirmations	p. 79
60-Day Guided Journal	p. 81
About The Author	p.143
A Gift, 4 Personal Development Exercises	p. 144
Personal Journal	p. 157

QUIT DRINKING

JOANNE EDMUND

THIS IS WHY THIS ALCOHOL ADDICTION RECOVERY WORKBOOK WAS WRITTEN FOR YOU

Life has become a routine, a destructive one. With evening, weekends, and days filled with people, fun, and drinks, you still feel alone - lonely actually - and miserable. Forgetting important dates, while desperately clinging to the minutes before the next drinks arrives, and constantly trying to hide your habit from friends. A cycle where drinking has become inevitable. Then you bought this book, because you wanted to cut off that cycle. You wanted a new life. A happy one. I wrote this book, because I know how it feels to be stuck in this seemingly, everlasting prison. To know that there is a way out, to believe in recovery, is hopefully the reason you bought this book. And the fact that recovery is possible, is why I wrote this book for you. Let's take this first step into your recovery journey together. I will tell you my story and my journey. Follow the exact steps or read it for mere inspiration. It's up to you. Take a deep breath…. And be proud you have taken the first step into the rest of your life.

***

JOANNE EDMUND

How to Use This Workbook

Throughout this workbook I am going to share what I did to overcome and understand my alcohol addiction. It was a journey with many bumps along the way, until I finally found a way to take control over my drinking, and my life. The practical step-to-step action plan in this workbook describes and explores my steps. Every step I took along my long road to recovery, I comprised into a daily exercise. By no means is this a 15-day workbook to overcome your alcoholism. But to work with daily exercises makes this workbook manageable. And to be true, recovery happens one day at a time. You could best use this workbook by reading it all through the end for the first time. Then, decide for yourself how you'd best like to use it. If I've learned one thing, it is that there is no cure-all for a drinking problem. So find your own. Be honest with yourself and take your necessary steps. The exercises throughout this workbook have been incredibly useful to me, and you can complete these exercises whenever you're ready. Use the Personal Journal at the end of this book to take notes of your recovery process. Over time, this Personal Journal will be an interesting and helpful guide in difficult times (My own Personal Journal became the inspiration and go-to source for this workbook). If you've bought the e-book, I recommend buying a notebook specifically for your recovery process.

Lastly, I would recommend to immediately start with the guided 60-Day Journal on page 81. These empowering writing prompts can help you with genuine and rigorous self-reflection on a daily basis. Making this journal a daily habit will benefit you immensely during recovery.

Let's turn to the next page, and take this journey forward.

JOANNE EDMUND

Introduction

"Between stimulus and response there is a space. In that space is our power to choose our response. In our response lies our growth and our freedom."

As human beings, we can choose how to react to addiction and recovery. I believe it doesn't matter whether you have been an alcoholic for a year or for your entire life. You always have the opportunity to change at this very moment. In every moment. Your response can change your life. The strategies explored in this workbook could serve as a tool against the urge to drink.

The steps in these five chapters had, and still have, amazing impact on my life. As part of my recovery process, I had some impressive insights that led me to discover that my whole life is not just my drinking problem. There is more to life than alcohol, than addiction. I found a new purpose to life, started to develop my God-given talents, to create a new, meaningful existence for myself and the people close to me. The light of this new life is sometimes overwhelming, but it has brought me true joy and love.

One step at a time, I started to enjoy the simple things once again. A smile, the kindness of my friends, and the love of my family. No more hiding, no more secrets, no more worrying about the stench of alcohol on my breath. It was a long road, but it took me to a place I had long forgotten to exist, life.

A purpose

No matter how bad life seems in this moment, it is never too late to start over. Nobody is destined to be miserable and tied indefinitely to an addiction. With time and effort even the worst situation becomes manageable, and over time will seem like a distant memory.

Your addiction is not your purpose, every human being is destined for so much more. First of all, to enjoy life, at least a tiny bit more.

I won't lie, this will be a difficult road, especially at first. You will need help and support to move along this road. Facing the unpleasant shadows of your past. But soon, you will also realize that this journey is worth each and every step. By purchasing this book you've realized a problem exists and the search for much-needed help has begun. However you use this book, my heart's cry to you is to acknowledge your problem, to be honest with yourself, and to drag your drinking problem into the light.

My Background

> I was drawn to all the wrong things: I liked to drink, I was lazy, I didn't have a god, politics, ideas, ideals. I was settled into nothingness; a kind of non-being, and I accepted it. I didn't make for an interesting person. I didn't want to be interesting, it was too hard. What I really wanted was only a soft, hazy space to live in, and to be left alone. On the other hand, when I got drunk I screamed, went crazy, got all out of hand. One kind of behavior didn't fit the other. I didn't care.
>
> **Charles Bukowski, Women**

I seemed like a typical kid, maybe a little too much of a tomboy, and spoiled as an only, adopted child. I was never truly happy. It happened when I was young, and at that time I thought it was normal. Being abused. I still remember it vividly, and half a bottle of gin. I was fourteen years old and didn't enjoy my very first drink. In fact, I puked after downing half a bottle with a few friends. It wasn't the only memory though, from drinking this hard liquor. For those few hours I forgot my nightmares, my past, my unhappiness.

A small town. That's where I grew up. Everyone knew everyone else, that kind of place. It was difficult to hide any behavior you did not want known. I was a teenager and, together with my best friend, I had a hard time gaining access to alcohol. Luckily, she lived in a gated community that rented fully stocked condos. We would watch a condo that was not currently rented. Predators hunting their prey. When no one was around we would break in and raid the liquor cabinets. No real damage to the condo, but the rush of breaking in made the alcohol taste even better.

This hunt for alcohol continued for about two years. Evenings and all weekend were spent getting drunk on cheap liquor with friends. I had quickly gotten to the point that I *had* to drink, I craved alcohol.

Then it happened, something to scare me straight.

I was joyfully sipping on a water bottle filled with Vodka. A typical day during my high school years. Then, the typical day took an unusual turn, the school had a drug dog show up unannounced. My heartbeat rose, and I tossed the bottle out the window. I'm not sure if anyone saw, but I was physically shaken the rest of the day. The next day, I knew I had to be more careful. But it wasn't the wake-up call I needed. The memory of the drug dog quickly faded, and I ignorantly continued to drink.

One morning, the abuse, the liquor cabinets, and the drug dog seemed of a distant past when I took a bunch of pills a friend had given me to 'relax' and chugged some vodka before my first class.

It changed my life.

By the second class I lost consciousness and passed out in the hall. I woke up in the hospital and my secret was out. At age sixteen I was put in a psych ward for a couple of weeks. It helped me to understand my basic problems, but the drinking problem wasn't properly addressed. Or I wasn't ready yet to confront it. By the time I got out, I was sober, and felt aware and at peace. It was blissful, and I stayed clean. For a few months.

***

A year later. I was seventeen years old and the party scene was enticing. Ready to graduate high school, the world was opening up. I headed to college and drinking was commonplace. Not just drinking, binge drinking. I spent weeks so drunk that I do not remember going to class.

My grades were okay, so no one cared.

I joined a sorority and things got worse. One night, in the middle of a blizzard, I was determined to get something to eat. I walked across campus in sandals and a white Adidas t-shirt for a sandwich.

Well, let's say, I did not get just the sandwich.

Friends had to come get me when campus security found me half frozen, but wanting to strip, while standing on a table in the middle of the campus restaurant. Drunk as hell. I needed alcohol like I needed air.

This continued through graduation. And then it continued while I had my first job. I knew I drank too much. There were times when I would cut back, but it never lasted long. Rock bottom hadn't arrived yet, and overconfident, I always thought I could have that second drink. And third. Until the ratio went out of the window and craving took over. I never fully realized how big of a problem I had. That is until the arrest.

Time for Change

Fifteen years after I took my first drink, the half-bottle of Gin, I was arrested. I was taken out of my home in handcuffs. Sirens wailed through the neighborhood. Neighbors were watching me. At that point I thought my life had ended. I spent a couple of months in jail, and was forced to clean up my act, since alcohol is not readily available when sitting in a cell. When I got out the cravings started right away. I was given two years of home confinement which meant no drinking in those two years. It should have been a blessing. And I made the most of it.

I didn't drink a single glass of alcohol in those two years.

Alcohol no longer was in charge. I thought I had turned the corner, but then I was released.

The Real Change

I started drinking again. Now in my thirties, unemployed, depressed, and forced to move back in with my mother. I felt embarrassed. My life was over as far as I was concerned. One morning I woke up sure it would be my last. I had no desire to live. Alcohol controlled my life 24/7, from craving, to the walk of shame into liquor stores, to the more and more lonely and heartbroken drinking episodes, until waking up and feeling like shit. Then, the cycle would repeat itself. I was trapped in an ongoing roller coaster, unable - actually unwilling - to take over the steering wheel.

"Why should I change?" I asked myself.

And I couldn't find an answer. I felt like nothing. On a whim, a last cry for help, I called a counseling center. A sweet, angelic voice answered. I cried. She was understanding, and she'd agreed to come by.

I still remember waiting in the dining room, drinking cheap, terrible red wine. My mother wasn't home. The bell rang. My alcohol suffered body staggered to the door. I was tipsy and rude, but she had dealt with others like me. She gave me the last push I needed to find lasting recovery. Through many books, therapies, journaling, and self-help I became sober. And that is what I want to share with you.

Through experience I can now confidently say, happiness cannot be found at the bottom of a bottle, as the saying goes, but it can be found within ourselves.

QUIT DRINKING

JOANNE EDMUND

The Recovery Workbook

*We either make ourselves miserable or we make ourselves strong.
The amount of work is the same.*

Carlos Castenada

CHAPTER 1 - THE FIRST STEP

These five chapters are the summary of my recovery process. Whether your addiction is as a daily drinker, a functional alcoholic, or a binge drinker, these chapters could benefit you.

Though it would help, you don't need a vision of your new life right now. Your first step is simple - but not easy - stop drinking. Stop being dependent on a substance that does not enhance your life. One step at a time. Taking small steps will be a worthwhile lesson as you learn to control and defeat your alcoholism for the rest of your life. Later in your recovery other life goals can be set.

Before my definite decision to stop drinking, I've had times of sobriety. It never lasted. What was positive though, during those short periods of sobriety, I learned new coping mechanisms for the times when I usually drank. New hobbies, positive self-talk, accountability, and healthy self-care all became useful weapons in my battle against alcohol.

The game changer for lasting recovery is both a practical plan to overcome your unhealthy drinking habit and a full understanding of *why* you are continuously pouring these glasses of alcohol.

We're not there yet. This is the beginning of the journey, the first step: to stop drinking. The rigorous and vital step, the gateway into an entirely different life. Try it for one day. Then for one week. And from then on all is possible. The following steps in the first chapter will help get you there:

Again, this is by no-means a 15-day workbook, but to make the steps into days makes it more understandable.

>
> **Day 1: Drag Your Secret Out Into the Light**
>
> **Day 2: Share Your Secret**
>
> **Day 3: Find An Accountability Partner**
>
> **Day 4: Interrupt the Drinking Pattern**
>
> **Day 5: Make An Emergency Plan**
>
> **Day 6: Celebrate**

Day 1: Drag Your Secret Out Into the Light

"Alcoholism is a devastating, potentially fatal disease. The primary symptom of having it is telling everyone – including yourself – that you are not an alcoholic."

H. Gravitz & J. Bowden, *Recovery: A Guide for Adult Children of Alcoholics*

The first day. A day without alcohol. A healthy day. Making it through this day means undeniably proving to yourself that you can get by without having a drink, and your journey towards lasting recovery can begin.

On this first day it is important that you drag your secret out into the light. To own your problem is the first step towards solving it. When I acknowledged my drinking problem for the first time I felt so much pain and hopelessness, yet at the same time this honesty also gave me the strength to seek a solution. When you open up about your drinking problem to yourself, no longer hiding for the truth, you will feel an immense relief. The beast inside you, craving for alcohol, will diminish in size once it is exposed to the warm light of the truth.

What could be helpful in admitting it to yourself, is understanding that you aren't the only alcoholic in this world. Many are, and many have successfully overcome their drinking habit.

Exercise

Your exercise for this day is to write a letter to yourself acknowledging your drinking problem, and also three reasons why you are committed to conquer the control alcohol has over your life. Think about those two things:

What pain do you want to avoid?

And what pleasure could you gain by quitting?

It could be a short letter, as long as it is an honest one that will give you hope and determination to continue your road to recovery. Make absolutely sure to save this letter. In later times, during your recovery, you can reread this letter and notice your progress.

Day 2: Share Your Secret

Congratulations! The first step has been taken! You've now walked through the gateway into a new life. Here, surrounded by a meaningful light, your drinking problem will no longer be a secret. No longer it will grow and haunt you in the dark.

Opening up about my addiction was something I dreaded for months, even years. And oh, how I wish now that I shared my secret earlier in my life. It would have saved me from severe problems and years of wasted time…

It happened one rainy afternoon, sitting in an old truck with a friend. Already, I had made quite a mess of my life, and the addiction chained me to a life of lying, stealing, and tearful hangovers. I knew what I had to do. The echoes of that old saying sung to me: the truth will set you free.

The truth.

In the truck I was silent, sweating, and bloody nervous. Until finally it all came out, from that very first bottle of gin to the drunken thief that I had become. There was silence. A non-judgmental silence in which I felt the eyes of my friend looking at me. I didn't dare to meet her gaze. At that moment, she first touched my hand, squeezed it, and then embraced me. I felt her kind-hearted spirit surround me. We talked for hours that day and she showed great love and concern. That moment gave me an enormous, almost spiritual strength to take the much-needed steps towards quitting drinking.

Exercise

Share your secret with another person. If you don't feel close enough to anyone, friends or family, then there are other options. For example, online alcoholic groups (where you could tell your story anonymously), Alcoholics Anonymous (AA) meetings held in nearly every town, or seeing a private therapist or religious counselor.

Sharing your secret for the first time is scary. But if you find the courage to do so, your dark and hideous secret will see the light and lose the power it once held.

If you find this step impossible, try practicing this moment of sharing your secret in the safety of your own house. Practice the conversation with yourself, in front of the mirror if possible, and do it for at least three days. Slowly you will build up the courage to take this necessary step. Remember, your situation, however horrific it is, is not unique. Thousands of recovered alcoholics before you have dealt with it and found the courage to take these much-needed first steps in their lasting recovery process.

Day 3: Find An Accountability Partner

Now that you have admitted to yourself and at least one other person that you have a drinking problem, the next step is to hold yourself accountable for your recovery process. This is especially difficult, because addiction has taught us that being secretive and lying is the way to get what we need. Again, this is not an easy road. Your best ally on this journey is the truth. It will loosen the grip of your addictive patterns. If you back telling the truth by an unbreakable will to avoid the pain of your drinking problem, and seek a life of true pleasure, plus the accountability that you will continue on your road to recovery even in the darkest of times, your chance of succeeding is almost certain.

Your accountability partner will very likely be the same as with whom you share your secret. Some months from now, in a brighter future, you will learn to trust yourself again. As it is supposed to be. Now, in the beginning, having a partner in your fight against the alcohol addiction could be vital for the likelihood of your success.

Exercise

Find an accountability partner. Besides an AA sponsor, other options could be a family member, a trusted friend, a life coach, a counselor, or an online therapy group. Do not attempt to take this journey all on your own. Even a little help could be the decisive factor in times when it's hard to continue.

Share with your partner what your goals are, total abstinence (highly recommended) or a more controlled drinking habit, and then make appointments on how you're going to stay in control for the first days, then the first weeks, of your recovery (the exercise on day 4 is helpful for making this plan). Share your likely pitfalls and make this person part of your road to recovery. Make decisions about when exactly, and how, you are going to check in and what it is you will discuss during these (short) sessions.

An accountability partner will only work if you are honest with yourself and with this person at all times. The goal of your partner should not be to judge, but to help.

Day 4: Interrupt the Drinking Pattern

Avoiding alcohol should be your aim during the first part of this journey. In short, it means interrupting the patterns that have led you to drinking in the past. If you had a favorite spot or a favorite store where you drank or bought alcohol, then this place should be avoided. Invent alternate routes so you will dodge these familiar places that hold hurtful memories and, likely enough, will trigger your drinking habit.

The same is true for people that inevitably lead you to a path of binge drinking. We all have these destructive drinking buddies. Cutting them off, at least for a while, is crucial if you want to stay sober in these first few weeks.

Furthermore, all alcohol should be removed from your home, as should all reminders of drinking. If you have a favorite glass, alcohol paraphernalia, or a favorite room that you spent time drinking in, then it is time for a change. Toss out any alcohol related items immediately. Rearrange your 'drinking room' and give it another purpose.

Lastly, trade in your drinking routine. Fill your nightly routine of cheap cans of beer and hard liquor with a healthy, pleasant, and *good* activity such as exercise, reading, or another hobby. Making small changes consistently will always lead to bigger changes in life.

Yes, I know these changes are hard. Finding and staying with a new routine takes effort and time. Just like becoming an alcoholic didn't happen overnight, lasting sobriety will not happen right away. Keep working at it moment by moment. One day, you will look back and realize it has been weeks since your last addictive thought of drinking.

Exercise

Write down the patterns that lead you to drink and write down a healthy alternative. Do this for places, specific times (at night, in the afternoon after coming home from work, etc.), and specific people. For example:

Place: *Liquor store close to my children's school*

Solution: *Take a different exit when I've dropped my kids to school, and drive by the park to sit down and read for a while.*

Day 5: Make An Emergency Plan

You could set your clock to it. In the first days, weeks, and months, the temptation to drink will arise. Tempted by an arty beer commercial, an old friend, or coincidentally stumbling upon your old drinking buddy. Life has a way of throwing us a curveball. What you need is a plan to escape.

Option 1: call your accountability partner. You could call your accountability partner if you find yourself craving alcohol, so they can talk you through the cravings and redirect you. If you are in a position that your support person cannot be contacted, then you need another plan.

Option 2: write down an emergency situation and how to overcome it. Visualize a period where your craving of alcohol starts. Write this down in detail. Then, visualize how you will beat this craving. Write this down in detail. Bring the situation and your solution together, first on paper then record it. This could be simply done on your phone. Listen to this situation and solution five times a day for seven days straight. Then for two weeks, listen to it daily. Slowly a hard-wired solution to beat your craving will form itself inside your mind.

Option 3: use an excuse to leave. Perhaps you run into a friend who is pressuring you to go to a bar to catch up on old times, what could you do? Have an excuse ready to get out of the situation. This doesn't have to be a lie, it can be a genuine excuse.

For example:

I am sorry I need to take off ... I have a project of my own and I have to work on it tonight. Shall we meet tomorrow morning for coffee?

Practice in front of the mirror so you won't get overwhelmed if the situation arises. Life happens, and we must be prepared to deal with things before they happen. To hammer it in, do not leave this excuse plan unpracticed.

Even though you are building up your defense mechanisms, you should never purposely put yourself in a situation just to gain practice. Remember, avoidance is best in the early stages of recovery.

Exercise

1. Write down your 'excuse-to-leave' and rehearse your plan on a daily basis for at least one week.
2. Discuss with your accountability partner if and how you could contact him or her in an emergency situation.
3. Do the visualization exercise as explained in option 2.

Day 6: Celebrate

A word of encouragement and compassion. As you first start your recovery, you may become painfully aware of all the heartache you have caused. A trail of unpleasant moments, to say the least. You may start blaming yourself for screwing up your own life, and the lives of others. Realizing the number of times you lied, intoxicated your body, and put others in difficult positions can be hard.

There will come a time when you will have to address these problems, but that time is not now. Now, it is time to deal with a life without drinking. That's work enough. In the early stages of recovery you must be your own cheerleader and best friend.

Take time to celebrate the enormous steps you've taken on the road to recovery:

- Acknowledging your problem
- Sharing your secret
- Finding an accountability partner
- Interrupting your drinking pattern
- Creating an emergency plan

Exercise

Celebrate your progress, your first steps on the road to lasting recovery. Write down at least five new, pleasant things that you could do now you've made the commitment to quit drinking.

For example:

- Instead of feeling miserable in the morning, meeting a friend for coffee.

- The $20 I spent daily to drink; every day $8 to pay off my debts, $4 to savings, and $8 in a fund for a nice holiday trip.
- Spending one hour every night working on a project I love, such as photography, playing tennis, dancing, acting, writing, or charity instead of binge drinking all night.

After you've done this write down at least three ways you could celebrate your recovery, and make sure to celebrate today! For example:

- Go to the movies with a friend
- Go to the bookstore and buy a book
- Visit family and have a nice dinner together

A last note to end this first chapter, it's essential to keep yourself positive and determined in this first stage of your recovery. Positive affirmations are magnificent for this. In no way is it about merely thinking positively and all becomes well. No. Your positive affirmations should reinforce the good work you're already doing, and the commitment and determination you have to realize lasting recovery.

At the end of this book I have added an extensive list of positive affirmations to keep you going. You could also write them down in your own words or use your own positive affirmations. Place these affirmations around your home, so they remind you every day of how you are taking back control of your life. Also, you could install an affirmation app so you will receive daily reminders on your smartphone. A free and helpful app is *My Affirmations*.

If you want to track your recovery progress, you can check out my just released new book: The Sobriety Journal,

www.amazon.com/dp/1726838765

Chapter 2 – Reconnect

"We repeat what we don't repair"

C. Langley-Obaugh

A Relapse?

If you've had a relapse, or even multiple relapses, DO NOT QUIT. Today is a new day. A new beginning. Relapse is common in all addictions and you're not alone in this. The recovery process is difficult, but never give up. Let these relapses be insightful lessons and stepping stones towards lasting recovery. It's useful to write down the patterns that lead to your relapse in your Personal Journal, so you know what to look out for and what to change in your life.

Chapter 1 is about making the downright commitment to quit drinking and how to work your way through the first stage of your recovery. All the things you learned in Chapter 1 shall prove to be powerful tools in the coming stages of your recovery.

Everyone with a drinking problem is resourceful to find ways to deceive and kid themselves into thinking that one or two drinks will not be a problem. As long as it is within reason...

There will be times when the urge seems insurmountable. All your good-hearted intentions are now seemingly overthrown by the craving for alcohol. Rather than giving up, it's in these moments you realize that this craving is the very problem. And recovery, with all its might and strength, is exactly your choice because, in time, it will overthrow the dependence for alcohol.

When you reconnect with yourself and your life again, a bigger purpose will slowly emerge. A goal, a vision, a future far away from intoxication. It will shine light over the shadows of your addiction.

Day 7: Start Enjoying Life Once Again

Day 8: Be Grateful and Proud

Day 9: Connect With Your Inner Voice

Day 7: Start Enjoying Life Once Again

Eliminating drinking will provide you with a significant amount of free time. No more hours spent in bars, or lonely hours drinking in the comfort of your own home with the curtains closed. As drinking dulls the senses and emotions, you may also find yourself feeling overwhelmed by these emotions, now floating to the surface. Anger and sadness are not uncommon in this period.

These overwhelming emotions are normal.

Your mind, spirit and body are going through an extreme emotional, physical, and mental cleanse. Your life has been lived through a drunken lens for many years in most cases. Reconnecting with your emotions, and also with the beauty that exists in the world, is new and undiscovered terrain. Use this free time and newly won awareness for something that feels joyful and gives you a sense of accomplishment.

Exercise

Create a new, satisfying habit. Find something you enjoy and do it on a consistent basis, so it becomes a new habit. In your Personal Journal write at least 7 things you've always wanted to do but lacked the time and energy for in the past because of your drinking problem.

Examples could be exercising, organizing a book club or a movie club, meditating, writing, designing clothes, joining a sports club, or creating an online business. Learn to enjoy the life you forgot you had. Choose at least one thing from your list and plan this activity in your calendar for the next two weeks.

It could be on a daily basis, or at least three times a week.

Day 8: Be Grateful and Proud

In Chapter 1, we discussed how to hold yourself accountable to someone else. It's time now to be your own guide and your own best friend. Recovery is tough and requires a strong support system and self-trust in order to be successful. To develop a new sense of self-esteem, it's best to start small. With being grateful and being proud.

Exercise

1. As you go through your day take at least one moment to find something to be grateful for in life. This could be your family or friends, a beautiful sunset, your job, your body, your house, a precious memory, anything. Write this down in your Personal Journal. In time you will acquire an extensive list of things, moments, and people you are grateful for in your life. On tough days, this list will show you how much you could be grateful for. It will soften the suffering. It's best to have this moment of gratitude at a specific time each day. Make it a habit. A good time to do this is in the morning, mid-day, or before you go to sleep.

2. Take a moment to reflect on something you're proud of. For example: a day without drinking, your progress on recovery, the lessons you have learned from a relapse, the kindness you showed to a stranger, and so on. Write this down as well in your Personal Journal to acquire a list of accomplishments you're proud of. Also make this reflection a habit.

This combination of gratitude and pride opens up a whole new road into self-acceptance, self-esteem, and self-confidence.

Day 9: Connect With Your Inner Voice

Note:

For those who are religious or want to be, it can be useful to engage in spiritual happenings such as church, prayers, or study groups. Where is written 'Inner Voice' in this paragraph, you could also change this for God, or another Higher Power you believe in.

First and foremost, you are not just an alcoholic; you are a human being capable of developing your talents, connecting with other human beings, and taking back control over your own mind and making your own decisions. To take back control it is crucial to reconnect with your Inner Voice. This does not require hours of meditation or years of study. It is simply a way of opening up to yourself and becoming your own best friend.

Through the use of honest, determined self-talk, affirmations, and gratitude your calm, strong, understanding and wise Inner Voice will speak again. Addiction has silenced this voice, through its destructive force and craving for alcohol. As if a tornado wiped out all the reasons within your mind and soul. As you learn to listen and trust your Inner Voice again, you can move out of this misery into a future you determine.

Exercise

Write down at least seven questions you know you have to ask yourself. For the next week, take the time to answer one of these questions per day. You could do this either through self-talk or journaling.

The weight of your answers will enhance when you do this in silence, give yourself a considerate amount of time to answer the question, and make the commitment to be honest. Slowly but surely, you will recognize that a wise voice will join your conversation, and in time, your Inner Voice will be a strong and trusted advisor once again.

Examples for questions:

What feeling(s) do I try to numb when I am drinking?

What feelings won't I allow myself to feel?

When were the moments in which I most craved a drink? And why was it in exactly these moments that I had to numb myself with alcohol?

For which actions in the past do I still struggle to forgive myself?

Is my self-pity true self-pity, or a mere escape to avoid addressing my real problems?

How would my life have looked if I'd never touched a glass of alcohol? And how could my life look if I never drank again?

What inside me do I fear? Now that I confront this fear, is it still so frightful? Why or why not?

***

Remember, you are moving in the right direction, all you have to do is keep going.

JOANNE EDMUND

Chapter 3 – Meet Your Addiction, A Trusted Advisor

"The first step toward recovery from alcoholism is the recognition that a problem exists. Once the problem drinker breaks through denial and admits to having a problem, a range of treatment options become available."

J. Nevid, *Health in the New Millennium*

So far you have taken time to admit your problem with alcohol, identified and interrupted your drinking pattern, created an *emergency plan*, learned a new habit and did some thorough soul searching. In chapter 3 we will delve deeper into the roots of your addiction. You will learn to respect and understand your addiction, without fearing it or falling into the trap again.

It is time to meet your addiction head on, look it straight in the eye. See it with clarity, and objectivity, and know your outcome: to master this force.

Day 10: Identify the Root of the Problem

Day 11: The Addiction Cue

Day 10: Identify the Root of the Problem

Today we will work to uncover your actual addiction. It's a process of picking apart this self-destructive ghost from the past in order to heal and make small steps forward. Only by truly facing the pain and fear that led to alcoholism, and understanding your addiction, will you genuinely find victory. Remember, you are not your addiction. You may be an alcoholic, but you are emphatically more than just a drinking problem.

Addiction is part of who we are and will always be part of us. We have to accept the power it holds over us. However, it does not control or define who we *can* be in life. As an example, you probably behave differently when drunk at a party than giving a presentation at work. We tend to adapt our personalities to the situation we are in each moment. Adapting means you could choose. Choosing the situation you're in, but more importantly, how you behave. This means you have an opportunity to create a better you.

***

In Day 9 you already worked with questions to uncover the truth about your hidden feelings. Today you will specifically question your addiction. The best place to start is always at the beginning and with the basics. If you are an alcoholic the basic question, that usually has a complex answer, is *Why do I drink?*

A host of answers and excuses will likely follow, until you dig deep enough... For me, it was the need to belong. Being part of a group, a family, friends, something, anything. When I drank, my borders were erased, and I felt the lightness to connect. And I forgot. Forgot everything. No more questions, no more sorrows, no more tears. Simply numb to all emotions.

As I explored these answers, a unified theme arose; I was running. I was running from myself and my emotions.

But why?

Why was I running? Why did I want to disappear? What made me so unhappy about myself? I discovered that I was still utterly upset with who I was, and with what was done to me as a child. Diving deep in the black ocean of hard liquor and cheap wine, drinking gave me a safeguard to escape the demons of abuse. I was a wounded child, and I wanted to forget about these wounds.

Unfortunately, drinking had masked any good feelings as well. I hurt the people I loved because I didn't want to be around those who could see through my drunken gaze. I wanted to protect my secret, and unconsciously, I knew that the people closest to me were my enemies. If they looked at me they would see, so I had to avoid them. It was too confrontational. It would remind me about myself, my potential, and how I was intoxicating my whole being.

***

By continuing to ask myself *why*, I was able to dig deeper and deeper into my true feelings, wants, and desires. I landed at the soul of my being. While drinking allowed me to relax and open up, even enjoy a few moments, it took away the things and people in life that mattered to me the most. Ruthlessly destroying the ties to everything I loved. Drinking, though unhealthy and destructive, was my comfort. I knew I had a problem. I knew drinking excessively was bad and dangerous, but I didn't care. Until I realized that the pain of continuing to drink was bigger than the pain of opening up about my addiction and taking the difficult steps to recovery.

When I made that choice, I took on the challenges that I had created for myself with a vigor that I didn't know existed.

I will not sugarcoat the journey. But each day, when I lack the motivation to step forward, I think about the past. That ugly, drunken, alcohol-stinking past. And I realize I've made the right choice. A conscious, living, and smiling present is now mine.

Making the journey inward to the roots of my addiction, looking back now, was what gave me the right foundation to help me even now, many years later, to stay on track.

Exercise

Important Note:

If you are in therapy, please discuss this step with your counselor or therapist as stated in the disclaimer of this book. This period, in all aspects, can be a very emotional time so be patient and caring with yourself and take on help from others (professionals) if you need to.

Today's exercise is about questioning your addiction. You will start with the following question, directed at the addictive part in yourself:

"Why do I have to drink to the point of destruction?"

You can answer this through self-talk or through journaling. To make the most out of this exercise, take your time and do it in a quiet place, as if it is an important ceremony. Don't be afraid, know that every part inside of you ultimately is under your control. Continue this questioning process, with three follow up questions. The only question you'll have to ask is 'Why?'

The process of this continuous *why* questioning will slowly but surely uncover the roots of your addiction. If you'd prefer - and I recommend this - you don't have to do this question process in one day. Take a full week to complete this exercise, and even ask more questions if it is required. Remember to jot down the most important insights in your Personal Journal.

***

Once more, I'll kindly notify you of the disclaimer in this book and at the beginning of this exercise.

Day 11: The Addiction Cue

It may seem backwards, but your current addiction served you to feel better. Drinking took away the pain, deep uncertainties, and fear you felt. At least, so it seemed. In reality, alcoholism only hid the feelings and allowed them to grow like weeds in the darkness of your soul.

The desire to drink may always be present. In time it will not be all-consuming, but the desire may pop up unexpectedly. Those are exactly the times you must explore why the desire has resurfaced. It usually means you are in a situation you wish to escape, or you feel bored, or need to numb your feelings. Instead of reactivating old, destructive habits use what you have learned so far, and with awareness, patience, and strength, guide yourself from the craving for alcohol to the solution of the real problem.

This way, you could use the *'addiction cue'*, as a reminder that something in your life needs attention.

Exercise

In today's exercise, we are going to make sure that alcohol is no longer your go-to option when the stressors of life rear their heads. In your Personal Journal, name at least five common reasons that activate your desire to drink. Try to describe them as accurately and specifically as possible. For example:

1. Being bored on Tuesday night because that's the night I am home alone and don't have any obligations.
2. Being anxious about my financial situation because my salary will hardly provide me with money to do nice

things. All money is used for necessities and paying off debts.
3. Being rejected, even in seemingly harmless situations, like a coworker who is not texting back. Or in more harmful situations, like an unfulfilling date.

Now, for every situation come up with at least two solutions that you could either say to yourself or do when these feelings arise. For example:

1. Join a sports club on Tuesday night. Meet up with a friend for a regular Tuesday movie night. In the moments I feel bored, practice with the questions in Day 9 and Day 10; before I do this, take five minutes to visualize how happy and confident I will be if I wake up sober tomorrow morning.
2. Make more realistic agreements with your creditors so you have a little more money to spend, and to save, each month. Listen to 20 minutes a day of a free audiobook on the subject of money, such as *The Richest Man In Babylon*. Come up with at least 3 possibilities to make 50 to 100 dollars more each month.
3. Ask yourself the question, "Am I a trusted, attractive partner to someone when I am a drunk?" Do a self-talk or journaling session with questions related to why you're feeling rejected. Visualize for 10 minutes, with your eyes closed and your favorite music on, how good of a friend, coworker, partner, single you could be if you stay sober and put in the time and energy to work on yourself and make yourself a better person.

Chapter 4 – A New Horizon

Only the shadows of the future were visible when you started this journey. Now, on Chapter 4 already, a new horizon has risen and is in plain view from your point in recovery. The past does not equal the future. The tremendous force of your drinking problem shivered, and passion for life has emerged. In this chapter, we will walk towards that new horizon, and towards creating a new life.

Day 12: Seek Inspiration

Day 13: Determine What You Want and Take Action

Day 12: Seek Inspiration

To stay on the right track and face adversity, inspiration is needed. We are always in control of how we respond to a situation. While we cannot necessarily control what life throws at us, our reaction can determine how things play out in a given situation. If we back our minds with a strong mental diet, it will be much easier to make the right choices.

While your singular goal at this point is to find peace and freedom from your alcoholism, you will need to move forward in other areas as well. This will mean further changes in other areas of your life. Reading inspirational books, watching motivational YouTube videos, personal coaching, and self-help programs could all be useful. Pushes in the right direction are how you create your new life.

Exercise

For at least three weeks go on a mental diet. Much like your body, your mind also needs the right kind of input to stay healthy and strong. This exercise is about taking in motivational, insightful, and positive content each day (preferably at the same time each day, so it can become a habit). For example:

- 20 minutes of reading inspirational non-fiction or fiction each day. (An extensive list of inspirational books is added at the end of this book.)
- 20 minutes of watching inspirational YouTube videos. (An extensive list of inspirational videos and YouTube channels is added at the end of this book.)

- Doing a self-help program on the internet or on an audio CD (An extensive list of self-help programs is added at the end of this book.)

If you want to take it a step further, hire a personal coach and work on your goals for specific areas of your life each or every other week.

Day 13: Determine What You Want and Take Action

Throughout this workbook you've worked on your life beyond alcoholism. During Day 12 we shook off the horrors of your drinking problem and dove into the sweet pool that is your new life.

When I became conscious for the first time in my life that all we have is 24 hours in a day, the same for me as for the Hollywood actress, the Grand Slam winner or the President of The United States, I felt an astounding power whirling up. I had been given the same opportunity as the greatest on this earth. Even if what I want is decidedly less glamorous than becoming a celebrity or a multimillionaire. Nevertheless, it is up to me to decide what I do with those 24 hours.

Exercise

Write down the 2-3 most important goals you have in your life right now. Write it down as a specific goal, or simply write down the area, such as family or career. For example:

1. Run a marathon next year
2. Family
3. Generate $1.000 per month through an online business this year

For each goal, write down at least seven actions you could take to come closer to achieving it or enhancing the quality of your life in that specific area. Act on one immediately. For example, if your goal is 'Family', call your parents tonight and check in on how they're doing. If your goal is generating $1,000 per month, claim a domain name and a host for your internet page today.

These small steps will develop into small victories. Slowly but surely, walking the path leading to the life you desire.

JOANNE EDMUND

Chapter 5 – A New Life

The final chapter. Escaping the jungle of shameful and drunken nights. Of lying and deceit. Of lost hope and gruesome regret. Standing tall on a new day. Making the commitment one day to never drink again. Relapses come and go, but what stays is the knowledge and a growing confidence that you will never surrender to your old choices. Accepting the power of your addiction but not giving in. Rising to the occasion, to face the struggle, face the fears, the painful insecurities, again and again, until you find the truth. The root. Then and there, your addiction wavers and you realize your power. Over it. Over everything inside of you. You see the new horizon, a glowing light, more beautiful than anything you've ever seen before. In the mirror you see a person with fresh eyes, self-confident and smiling, and before long you will realize the weeks, the months, the years of fighting were all worth it. You realize the mighty, beautiful person looking back at you in the mirror, is you.

Day 14: Don't Get Overconfident

Day 15: Commit to Your New Life

Day 14: Don't Get Overconfident

If you've come this far on your road to recovery, it's easy to overestimate your abilities. What harm will it do to go to that bar, if I know I'll only drink a beer? What harm will it do to meet my old drinking buddy again? What harm will it do to forget my new, constructive habits for a couple of days in a row? What harm will it do if I have just one drink…

Throughout your recovery, remember this one sentence:

> *"The best friend to relapse is overconfidence."*

Exercise

Find three of your weak spots and practice your solution to each of these for at least one week. Go back into your Personal Journal, or have a good self-talk, to determine your three weak spots in your recovery process. Maybe you've felt tempted to drink, now or in the past, when you're anxious about your financial situation, when someone rejects you, or simply when you think it's all going *too well* in your life. Yes, *too well*. Sometimes, to stay in our comfort zone, we even try to sabotage our successes.

Write down at least three weak spots and your three determined solutions to these weak spots, whenever they arise. Practice these three solutions for at least one week, either through rewriting the solution each day or visualizing the solution.

Day 15: Commit to Your New Life

We started this workbook by writing a letter. It was in that letter that you had to admit your drinking problem to yourself. This may seem like a lifetime ago. Seasons have passed and the color on your face is rich and glowing. Standing where you are today, it will feel like a reward to look back. To track your progress. To see where you were and where you have come. To realize that so much is possible when you admit your weaknesses, and find and use your strengths.

Exercise

Reread your letter from Exercise 1 and destroy it. The past is the past. Then, write a new letter to your future self, one year from now. Write about your journey and how proud you are today and write about what you would like to accomplish one year from now. Commit to your new life in this letter. Do this exercise with care and attention.

Here on you let the past be the past and commit to your new life.

JOANNE EDMUND

Epilogue

Nearly ten years ago I was sitting in a jail cell, wondering if these were the walls that would deprive me of my last hope for happiness. But it wasn't the end. I got out, but the truth didn't set in right away. In fact, it took me another eight years to realize that most of my problems started with drinking. Now, three years after my last drink, I can honestly and proudly say I am content with my life.

It's good now.

I am improving my life day by day. I have a job and considerate friends that truly love me. I have made amends with family members and said goodbye to many who weren't good for me.

Most of all, I've begun to accept and love myself again.

Alcoholism took away my pride, my ability to love, and my ability to feel. Recovery has brought all of it back. The mighty waves of addiction weren't enough to drown me. The water has become calm and steady again.

Now, I can go out with friends and enjoy the occasional night out without drinking alcohol. Other, healthy and *good* habits have emerged and replaced the old, destructive ones. When I am at work, I don't worry about getting my next drink immediately when I'm off, or when I am alone in the office and my bottle of whisky is waiting in the drawer. I've stopped shaking when I am not drinking. The restlessness has slowly disappeared. I feel good and proud, my body is healthier, and I have found a life outside of drinking again.

These are the last sentences, the last words I write to you. While seeing the word-filled pages on my laptop I am thinking about you, the reader. About your situation and your pain. For a brief moment, I feel connected to someone I don't know. Someone that doesn't know me, and is reading my story. My steps towards recovery.

I think, I hope, and I pray that you, above all else, you have gained the inspiration you needed from my story. Wake up from your nightmare, don't forget to breathe, and find and embrace the life that is waiting for you.

One More Thing

I am a beginning author and need all the help you can offer me. My gratitude to you, for buying this book with your hard-earned money and giving a beginning author, your faith, means the world to me.

To help me spread the word for this book, would you take a few seconds and leave me a review on Amazon and/or Goodreads? The most important part of how well a book sells is how many positive reviews it has, so if you leave me one then you are directly helping me to continue on this journey as a full-time writer.

Thanks in advance to anyone who does. It means a lot.

Sincerely yours.

JOANNE EDMUND

Book Recommendations

Listed on the following pages are several books and videos that have helped me through my journey.

Man's Search for Meaning by Viktor Frankl

Portrait of an Addict as a Young Man by Bill Clegg

Who Moved My Cheese? by Spencer Johnson M.D.

The Addiction Recovery Workbook by C.W. V. Straaten

The Power of Habit by Charles Duhigg

Unshakeable by Anthony Robbins

How to Quit Drinking Without AA by Jerry Dorsman

The Truth by Neil Strauss

The Gift of Sobriety by Marc Allen

The 5 Second Rule by Mel Robbins

This Naked Mind Control Alcohol by Annie Grace

Dying to Survive: Surviving Drug Addiction: A Personal Journey through Drug Addiction by Rachael Keogh

The Presence Process by Michael Brown

Video Recommendations

Why We Do What We Do by Tony Robbins (TED Talk)

https://www.ted.com/talks/tony_robbins_asks_why_we_do_what_we_do

How to Stop Screwing Yourself Over by Mel Robbins (TEDX)

https://www.youtube.com/watch?v=Lp7E973zozc

Everything You Think You Know About Addiction is Wrong by Johann Hari (TED Talk)

https://www.ted.com/talks/johann_hari_everything_you_think_you_know_about_addiction_is_wrong

Narratives of seven women recovering from problems with alcohol

https://www.youtube.com/watch?v=N0X2aRnYL4E

Risky Drinking, HBO Documentary

https://www.youtube.com/watch?v=4hKmYthx718

Woman Reveals How She Pulled Herself Back From Alcoholism

https://www.youtube.com/watch?v=_MBwgGm5hT0

How to Stop Drinking Alcohol, Tips & Motivation by James Swanwick

https://www.youtube.com/watch?v=A-mjhtADLBo

Stop Your Addiction, Most Incredible Advice by Tony Robbins

https://www.youtube.com/watch?v=PNeystiamgg

Best AA Speech Ever

https://www.youtube.com/watch?v=AekbQ2ye3o8

Quotes

"Between stimulus and response there is a space. In that space is our power to choose our response. In our response lies our growth and our freedom." – Viktor Frankl

I have walked out of the darkness and into a light that is sometimes overwhelming, but one that has brought true joy and love into my life. – Unknown

"I was drawn to all the wrong things: I liked to drink, I was lazy, I didn't have a god, politics, ideas, ideals. I was settled into nothingness; a kind of non-being, and I accepted it. I didn't make for an interesting person. I didn't want to be interesting, it was too hard. What I really wanted was only a soft, hazy space to live in, and to be left alone. On the other hand, when I got drunk I screamed, went crazy, got all out of hand. One kind of behavior didn't fit the other. I didn't care." – C. Bukowski

"If you have made mistakes, there is always another chance for you. You may have a fresh start any moment you choose, for this thing we call 'failure' is not the falling down, but the staying down." — Mary Pickford

"Alcoholism is a devastating, potentially fatal disease. The primary symptom of having it is telling everyone – including yourself – that you are not an alcoholic."   -H. Gravitz & J. Bowden

"We either make ourselves miserable or we make ourselves strong. The amount of work is the same." -C. Castenada

For all sad words of tongue and pen, the saddest are these, 'It might have been'. — John Greenleaf Whittier

"We repeat what we don't repair" -C. Langley-Obaugh

Expect the dawn of a new beginning in the dark nights of life. — Lloyd John Ogilvie

"The first step toward recovery from alcoholism is the recognition that a problem exists. Once the problem drinker breaks through denial and admits to having a problem, a range of treatment options become available." -J. Nevid

When everything seems like an uphill struggle, just think of the view from the top. - Unknown

Affirmations

These affirmations can help you to change your beliefs around self-confidence, cravings, recovery and self-esteem for the better. You could also write them down in your own words or use your own positive affirmations. Place these affirmations around your home, so they remind you every day of how you are taking back control of your life. Also, you could install an affirmation app so you will receive daily reminders on your smartphone. A free and helpful app is *My Affirmations*.

"I take time to see, sense and imagine myself confident, proud of myself, and sober each day."

"It will be great to wake up being free of a hangover, guilt from a binge drinking episode, or a foggy brain."

"I choose to move away from alcohol"

"I know I will be proud of myself when I'm sober"

"I will be so much more successful when I quit drinking"

"I am beginning to forgive others for the hurt they have caused me"

"My soul, body and mind will feel better immediately when I stop using alcohol."

"I am beginning to forgive myself for any wrongs I have committed in the past."

"I am worth my own self-love, self-acceptance."

"I am learning to love and accept myself just as I am."

"I express my needs, feelings, and communicate them in a respectful manner."

"I rely on my inner gut feelings, to help guide me towards the life I want to live."

"I am NOT a victim, I am an empowered person."

"I intend to live each day in joy–and to appreciate the pleasure in the present moment."

"I am creating exciting things to do that are not related to alcohol."

60-Day Guided Journal

With this 60-Day guided journal, you can genuinely question the causes of addiction, find out how to deal with fear, insecurities & anxiety, and determine your real purpose in life. Making journaling a daily habit in general, has fantastic benefits. I would personally say that journaling now is one of my favorite personal development exercises. It helps me to discover new ideas, reflect on my worries, and cultivate an attitude of positivity and gratitude towards life. To help you start your journaling habit, and to help you to reflect on your addiction and other issues in life, This 60-Day Journal is created from my one-year journal *Happy & Sober* My recommendation is to set a specific time each day where you use this journal. For example, during your morning routine or evening routine.

Also, I've created two journals you can use on a daily basis. If you seriously want to integrate daily journaling, these books might be of interest to you. You can find them on my Amazon author's page,

http://www.amazon.com/Joanne-Edmund/e/B07GNVTV8Q

Day 1 - What advice would you give someone else when it comes to dealing with insecurities during sobriety?

Day 2 - What is the best response to deal with the thought: "Sobriety is boring."

Day 3 - What events have inspired you to take the steps to quit drinking?

Day 4 - If your addiction was a person, what would be his or her characteristics?

Day 5 - Write a description of an ideal day in your life one year from now.

QUIT DRINKING

Day 6 - Write down three solutions to make your recovery progress more enjoyable.

Day 7 - Why do you feel grateful for being in recovery this week?

Day 8 - Write down a slogan, or a few sentences that encourages recovering alcoholics to stay sober.

Day 9 - How would you respond strongly and kindly to yourself when this thought arises: "I can easily drink just one glass per day"?

Day 10 - What about life did you once believe, but not anymore? Why?

Day 11 - If your addiction was a person, what would his or her physical appearance be?

Day 12 - Write down five things you appreciate when it comes to your relationship with The Universe/God/Your Creator.

Day 13 - When it comes to your sobriety process, what progression would you love to make one month from now?

QUIT DRINKING

Day 14 - What thought(s) irritated you this week?

Day 15 - What would be the best way to deal with a relapse?

Day 16 - Write three easy solutions to prevent a relapse.

Day 17 - Write three affirmations that will lower your fear of a relapse.

Day 18 - What is your weak spot when it comes to an unhealthy relationship?

Day 19 - Write down five things you appreciate when it comes to your relationship with yourself.

Day 20 - What about love did you once believe, but not anymore? Why?

Day 21 - What about other people did you once fear, but now feel neutral or joyful toward?

Day 22 - What was your secret pay-off for continuing drinking while knowing you were addicted?

Day 23 - If you could ask your 80-year-old self one question, what would it be? What would be the answer?

QUIT DRINKING

Day 24 - Write one affirmation to live by today.

Day 25 - What thoughts often make you smile? Why?

Day 26 - How has your relationship with your family affected your sobriety positively?

Day 27 - How has your relationship with your family affected your sobriety negatively?

Day 28 - Describe the moment you realized you were addicted to alcohol.

Day 29 - What advice would you give your younger self when it comes to friendship?

QUIT DRINKING

Day 30 - How can your inner child help you during your recovery process?

Day 31 - How would you describe your alcoholism to your parents?

Day 32 - What you would love to see if you only had two more months to live?

Day 33 - What you would love to say if you only had two more months to live?

Day 34 - How can your higher self help you during your recovery process?

Day 35 - How would the people closest to you describe you during your alcoholism periods?

Day 36 - What about friendships did you once fear, but now feel neutral or joyful toward?

Day 37 - What thought(s) irritated you today?

Day 38 - Describe the force of alcoholism.

Day 39 - Try to meditate today for three minutes. You can do this with a free guided meditation on YouTube or just set your alarm. Afterward, write down a reflection.

Day 40 - How can you improve your integrity on a daily basis?

Day 41 - Write down five things you're fascinated by when it comes to health.

Day 42 - When it comes to your sobriety process, what progression would you love to make three days from now?

Day 43 - Write one affirmation to live by this week. And explain why you choose for it.

Day 44 - What are your thoughts on the use of accountability during your sobriety process?

Day 45 - What are your thoughts on the influence of alcohol in modern western society?

Day 46 - What is a small thing you can do today to improve your relationship with yourself?

Day 47 - Who would you like to learn from when it comes to sobriety? Why?

Day 48 - What are the things you would love to say to your younger self that was buried in the heaviness of alcoholism?

Day 49 - If *recovery* was a person, what would he or she look like?

Day 50 - If *recovery* was a person, what would his or her characteristics be?

Day 51 - What about The Universe/God/Your Creator did you once believe, but not anymore? Why?

Day 52 - If you could ask your future self, one year from now, one question, what would it be? What would be the answer?

Day 53 - What about money did you once like, but now dislike?

Day 54 - Why is self-reflection important?

Day 55 - How does your ideal week look?

Day 56 - Who would you like to learn from when it comes to personal growth? Why?

Day 57 - When it comes to your sobriety process, what progression would you love to make one week from now?

Day 58 - What would your ideal situation look like when it comes to your recovery process?

Day 59 - How can humor help you during recovery?

Day 60 - When it comes to your relationship with your friends, what progression would you love to make one year from now?

This is the end of this 60-Day Journal. If you want a one-year version, you can buy my book *Happy & Sober, 365 Questions For Recovery,* here,

www.amazon.com/dp/1688699562

About the author

Joanne Edmund is the pen name of a former alcoholic, who would like to keep her name to herself, to protect the people who are close to her. After years of battling the horrors of alcoholism and destroying her life and the lives of others, she hit rock bottom. After jail time, and through a great deal of soul searching, therapy, and AA, she found sobriety. Her dream in early childhood was to become a writer of fantasy fiction. As a middle-aged woman she finally fulfilled her dream to become an author. Not writing fiction, but her story of recovery.

In her most daring dreams, she hopes this workbook can inspire hundreds of thousands of alcoholics around the world and through the years.

Her new book *The Sobriety Journal* is out now on Amazon, www.amazon.com/dp/1726838765

About *The Sobriety Journal*,
The best & simplest self-help method to enjoy gratitude, learning, and happiness in your daily life. A sober journal created by someone in recovery. Step by step towards lasting sobriety. No intimidating questions or big commitments, but a remarkable way to experience your day by day recovery and make it truly life-changing. With as little as five minutes each morning and night, you will create a powerful journaling habit.

Begin your day at the right footing and calm down your monkey mind with daily reflections. In recovery, we all know that life can be seriously tough. Give your experiences a lifelong purpose by writing them down in The Sobriety Journal, and thus making your very own, personal, go-to guide for lessons from the past.

A Gift

On the following pages, 4 Exercises for Self-Growth from the acclaimed Self-Help Workbook:

21 Exercises For Self-Growth *A Life- Changing Workbook*

These exercises have helped me personally and I hope they will do the same for you.

For sale on Amazon.com

(www.amazon.com/Personal-Development-Secrets-Exercises-Reliance-ebook/dp/B0737G1ZWK)

Don't Waste Your Talents, Live Your Passion

Exercise 1: Spend at least 30 minutes a day this week on something you absolutely love

The responsibilities of everyday life frequently interfere with our most enchanting dreams and our real talents. With a thousand things to do, it's normal to wonder where the time has gone. One day you are 21, and then suddenly—in the blink of an eye—you are in your mid-thirties. Sometimes it feels impossible to cope with time. Where are the dreams you've had when you were 12-years-old and life seemed easy with no restrictions?

> *"There is no passion to be found playing small - in settling for a life that is less than the one you are capable of living."*
> Nelson Mandela (1918-2013)

Tap Into Your Greatest Strengths
Your unique talents and callings will never be erased. Maybe you feel the calling to blow off the dust from your old dreams and thrive in ways you would have never imagined. Being a better parent, becoming a novelist, being a contributor to the poor and undeveloped in this world, starting your own business or finally having that loving relationship you have longed for. And the good thing is? Living your true passion can start as soon as today. This is not a cheesy marketing line. This is the truth.

Whenever we tap into our greatest strengths and our biggest dreams, something amazing happens. A new flow of life-energy is released through you and goes out into the world. For those of you who have a true passion but are stuck waiting for the right moment to take action or, even worse, think your dreams are unrealistic, there is but one piece of advice: start today!

But...
We hear you thinking. My job, my family, my character, my debts, my age, my study, my, my, my. Don't you believe you were put on this Earth to do the absolute most with your time and unique talents? Chase that calling and fight for what you want. Think about these questions and be honest about your answers. Remember that it's not too late; the best time to start is always right now.

Adversity
If you've taken the first step already, you know how good it feels to be on the path of following your dreams, challenging your talents and living with passion. However, while it's nice at first, adversity can set in. After a couple of days, or weeks, or months. That's the first price you have to pay when you are on this freeing path. Still, we urge you to fight your limiting beliefs and negative thoughts—and don't forget to ignore the negativity from other people. It will be there, too.

This is why we encourage you to take small but consistent steps. Make it a habit of spending a little bit of time per day on something you're passionate about. At first, it could be as small as thirty minutes. This way, you will become more used to this new activity of doing something you're passionate about. You will build up a defense that will benefit you whenever adversity sets in.

Dreams can always change. That's part of life. It's not a fundamental "must" to achieve your dreams, but we think it is a must to be on the journey toward your dreams. Try. That is self growth. Commit to something you're passionate about—it's part of this journey.

Exercise 1

We invite you to make this a week where you tap into your greatest strengths and biggest dreams. The exercise is to spend at least 30 minutes a day for one week on something you absolutely love. If you are already doing so, try to give yourself even more time per week on learning your particular craft. Whether you do it for seven straight days or decide to skip the weekend, that's up to you. Here are five examples for this exercise:

Examples:

- If you want to become a better parent, read a book on parenting every day and plan quality time with your children at least three times a week
- If you want to become a novelist, you could start with structuring the outlines for your future novel for 30 minutes a day
- If you want to build your own business, research your niche and come up with at least 10 actions you could take to kick-start your business
- If you want a loving relationship, read books on dating advice or join dating apps and websites
- If you are passionate about being more self-confident and want to shed some weight, commit to working out and drinking more water instead of sodas and alcohol for a week

Tip: An outstanding book on tapping into your great strength is *The Big Leap* by Gay Hendricks. In this book, he explains in detail how to live in your "zone of genius." The book is also available as an audiobook.

Say Hello To Yourself

Exercise 2: Connect With Your Inner Wisdom

The second exercise in this book will be one that works as fuel for other exercises. Connecting with your inner wisdom is vital if you want to improve yourself. It's the connection to the wise, strong, endlessly loving and always understanding part of ourselves that can guide us through dark and difficult times. This higher self will support you to achieve your greatest goals. We all have this voice of inner wisdom. No matter what your current life situation is, it can fight for you. When you use your inner strengths, self growth will be your default setting.

Note: In this book, we will use both "higher self" and "inner wisdom" as an equal term.

> *"When you operate from the Higher Self, you feel centered and abundant— in fact, overflowing. When you experience this abundance, your fears automatically disappear."*
> Susan Jeffers author of *Feel The Fear And Do It Anyway*

Different Parts
It's essential to recognize that we could operate from different parts of ourselves. For instance, when you eat chips on a couch while watching a reality show out of procrastination, you act from a different personal part of yourself than when you give a killer presentation at work. Fear, excitement, and other emotions, together with thoughts and external situations, lead to different behaviors from different parts of ourselves. Our higher self is often overlooked. Between our worries and other toxic thoughts, this part hardly gets a chance to be your own wise counselor.

Fortunately, this inner wisdom remains no matter what. You can connect to it wherever and whenever you want to. If you haven't ever done so, or haven't for a very long time, it will take more effort. No matter what, though, your own personal counselor is ready to serve you.

Self-talk & Silence
Through self-talk and silence, you can connect with your inner wisdom. You can hear your higher self when you pay close attention or ask direct questions. For religious people, this might feel like a spiritual experience. If you aren't religious, connecting with your higher self is just as important and possible for you. See it as your inner infinite wisdom. In times of stress, tough decisions and suffering, this inner wisdom gives a sense of comfort, calmness, peace, and encouragement. Let it guide you toward the creativity that leads to new solutions, astounding ideas and great artistic work.

Perhaps the concept of self-talk sounds strange, mystical or even comes across as utter nonsense to you. Whatever the case may be, we invite you to try this exercise with an open mind. It's extremely important to bond with yourself in order to improve yourself. Be your own best friend and trust the process.

The most helpful approach to doing this is by connecting with your inner wisdom.

You will find an incredible wisdom inside of yourself that can lead to a sense of calm. Although worries, pain, and fear may not dissolve entirely or even quickly, it will help you find a solution to problems—or perhaps even the power to accept difficult situations in life for what they are.

Exercise 2

Connect at least once a week for one month with your inner wisdom. Determine a part of life where you have worries. Recognize and accept it, then go to a peaceful place in your house or out in nature. Give yourself some time to slow your thoughts down. Then, ask this question: I worry about _____ situation, can you give me advice on how to deal with it?

Do a session of at least 15 minutes. Use the first 5 minutes to slow down your thoughts. Meditation is suggested here. Then ask your question and start a self-talk. If you don't get anywhere the first time, don't worry! Try again next week. Sometimes it takes time to connect with your higher self, especially when you're not used to doing so.

Tip: If self-talk and inner wisdom sounds odd to you, keep it light and fun while you try this exercise. Nobody will judge you, so don't worry about that. Just give it a try and maybe you will surprise yourself.

Be A Worry-Solver

Exercise 3: Make a list of worries in your life, then take action by solving one immediately

The opposite of self growth is being imprisoned by negativity and worries. When you let them, worries can occupy your mind 24/7. They will be the rulers of your empire and you will be a mere slave. While there are concerns in life, our worries typically are about situations yet to come or worries about the past. You do not know what the future holds and you cannot change your past, so why punish yourself? The famous Mark Twain quote is a guideline to live by.

> *"I've had a lot of worries in my life, most of which never happened."*
> Samuel Langhorne Clemens, "Mark Twain", American author (1835 - 1910)

It's Not All About Positivity

Is it all about positivity? No, that's way too easy. Horrible things can and do happen in life. There are plenty of real concerns to consider. But, we can deal with these concerns in two ways. We can either accept them or make a change. Worrying has never solved any problem. However, thinking about solutions and consciously acting does.

Now, focus on your worries for a moment.

Yes, they're but mere thoughts. Nothing more and nothing less.

We can't predict the future and we can't alter the past. We realize that this is way easier said than done. Yet, you owe it to yourself to at least practice this way of thinking and living. Start with seeing your worries for what they are: thoughts. Creations from the fearful part of your mind.

Accept or Change
We will say it again, either accept your concerns or change your situation. You could worry about your financial situation, relationship, health, weight or any other concern, but it won't go away by obsessing over it!

Accept the flaws of your partner or sit down for a heart to heart talk. Accept your body for what it is or exercise and stay away from fast food. Accept that in your current situation you can't make time for your artistic dreams or spend at least 45 minutes a day on your writing. Don't worry—just accept or change the situation.

Exercise 3

Make a list of worries in your life and take action by solving one immediately. Get in the habit of confronting and solving concerns promptly. In this exercise, you will make extensive lists of all your current worries. Think about all the areas in your life and what, specifically, makes you anxious.

Step two is to look at the list. If you see these worries on paper, are they still real worries? Maybe you can scrape off a couple worries already.

The last step is picking one worry and either solving the problem immediately or starting the process of acceptance. Try to get into the habit of either accepting or solving your concerns directly when they arrive. As we said earlier, this is way easier said than done, but it is more than worthy to be heroic and escape your prison of worries.

Tip: The book *The Way of the Peaceful Warrior* by Dan Millman is a fascinating and inspiring story about how to live in the "here and now" instead of allowing worries to control your life. The audiobook version of the book is done by the author himself. Also, the book has been made into a movie of the same name.

Your Own Ideal Vision

Exercise 4: What's your ideal vision for your own life? Dare to dream big and put it on paper!

Self growth begins with knowing what you want. What's your direction in life? We sometimes feel the pressure to make something out of our lives—and that's normal. However, without a clear direction, stress comes in and it's hard to ignore. What do I want from my brief time on this Earth?

Our lives never stay the same permanently. Peaks and valleys, remember? While fluctuation in life is normal, you don't want to catch yourself in a downward spiral for decades, years, or even months. Take matters into your own hands and determine your course.

> *"We are haunted by an ideal life, and it is because we have within us the beginning and the possibility of it."*
> Phillips Brooks, American Preacher (1835-1893)

Express yourself without limit
A compelling vision is a driving force for all of our goals. There should be no hesitations and no limitations when you write this vision. It's just on paper for now, but who knows? Dreams can come true, right? This is similar to the previous exercise: Express yourself without limit. Instead of singing and dancing, now it's about writing all your deepest desires and biggest hopes. Being a millionaire, building an AIDS-hospital in Africa, traveling through the southern parts of Asia, having a family or driving a Lamborghini—it's up to you!

What we want to create in this exercise is a compelling vision that is truly yours and one that is more or less realistically achievable. Do you dream of being a millionaire but at the moment you're dead broke? That's okay; we still think the dream is absolutely achievable. Just read the stories of self-made millionaires. One guru in the 'becoming rich niche' and also a multimillionaire himself, T. Harv Eker, began as a broke young man coming who moved back in with his parents three times before becoming successful.

Endless Possibilities
There are endless possibilities as long as you have a plan, the determination, and the persistence to take consistent action toward your vision. In the next two exercises, we will break your ideal vision up into achievable goals for the foreseeable future. You will make a game plan and take instant action.

For now, there is no time limit. Dream big and write your compelling vision.

Think about the purpose behind your big vision. WHY do you want to have a family? WHY do you want to become a millionaire? WHY do you want to build a hospital in third-world countries? Your purpose is the driving force behind your ideal vision. It stands side by side with your values in life.

Exercise 4

Make a compelling, ideal vision for your life and write it down. You could also add photos (from your ideal house, bank account, family picture, audience, etc.) to conceptualize your ideal vision. When you're ready, try to visualize yourself in your ideal life. How would you feel? How would you look? How would you behave?

Tip: Set up a weekly or monthly event in your calendar to check your ideal vision. Your ideal vision could change overtime. In the next exercise, we'll dive deeper into being flexible enough to alter your goals and vision whenever life, or a change in what you're passionate about, calls for it.

QUIT DRINKING

Personal Journal

QUIT DRINKING

QUIT DRINKING

QUIT DRINKING

QUIT DRINKING

QUIT DRINKING

JOANNE EDMUND

QUIT DRINKING

JOANNE EDMUND

QUIT DRINKING

JOANNE EDMUND

QUIT DRINKING

JOANNE EDMUND

QUIT DRINKING

QUIT DRINKING

QUIT DRINKING

JOANNE EDMUND

QUIT DRINKING

An Inspiring Recovery Workbook by a Former Alcoholic

BY

JOANNE EDMUND

2018

Printed in Great Britain
by Amazon